CW00969956

Project Management
Body of Knowledge

Association for Project Management

Project Management

Body of Knowledge

Fourth Edition

Edited by **Miles Dixon**

on behalf of APM's Professional Board

Acknowledgements   The Association for Project Management (APM) wishes to acknowledge the research commissioned by APM and conducted under the direction of Professor PGW Morris by the Centre for Research in the Management of Projects, UMIST. This research was sponsored by BNFL, Unisys, Unicom, GEC Dunchurch and Duhig Berry Ltd. The Association also wishes to place on record its appreciation of the fundamental work carried out over a period of years by the late Brain Willis OBE

e-mail   Secretariat@apm-uk.demon.co.uk
web site   www.apm.org.uk

ISBN   1-903494-00-1

Designed and typeset by Cambridge Publishing Management, 149B Histon Road, Cambridge, CB4 3JD, England, a division of G&E 2000 Limited

Printed and bound in the UK for APM by G&E 2000 Limited A1 Parkway, Southgate Way, Orton Southgate, Peterborough, PE2 6YN

Contents

Preface

The Association for Project Management (APM) first began developing a Body of Knowledge in the late eighties, with the first edition being published in 1992. While there have been a number of updates since then, this is the first fundamental revision the Association has undertaken.

This new edition was commissioned because project management is changing, and the body of knowledge needs to reflect this.

The prime input for this new edition was a research project undertaken by the Centre for Research into the Management of Projects at the University of Manchester's Institute of Science and Technology, co-sponsored by the APM,[1] and led by Professor Peter Morris. The importance of this research was that it carried out an independent survey of the practice of project management in relation to the elements of knowledge that project management professionals in a range of industries felt they needed.

This Body of Knowledge is thus a practical document, defining the broad range of knowledge that the discipline of project management encompasses. It is not however a set of competencies, nor does it say much about the behavioural characteristics that are important in project management. Indeed, to be successful as a project management practitioner requires a combination of the right knowledge (allied to personal experience) and attitude (or behaviour). An indication of important behavioural characteristics is given on the next page.

The APM, together with many other organisations, uses its Body of Knowledge as the basis for its various professional development programmes. As continuity in such programmes is vital, a comparison to the topics in the previous version is given at the end of this document.

Behavioural Characteristics of Project Management Professionals

Characteristics of an individual's personality generally recognised as important in project management are:

1 The full report on the research can be obtained from UMIST or via the APM

- **Attitude** – an open positive "can do" attitude which encourages communication and motivation, and fosters co-operation.
- **Common sense** – the ability to spot sensible, effective, straight forward, least risky, least complex solutions i.e. 90% right on time is better than 100% far too late!
- **Open mindedness** – an approach where one is always open to new ideas, practices and methods and in particular gives equal weight to the various disciplines involved on the project.
- **Adaptability** – a propensity to be flexible where necessary and avoid rigid patterns of thinking or behaviour, to adapt to the requirements of the project, the needs of the sponsors, its environment and people working on it – to ensure a successful outcome.
- **Inventiveness** – an ability to discover innovative strategies and solutions from within oneself or by encouragement with other members of the project team, and to identify ways of working with disparate resources to achieve project objectives.
- **Prudent risk taker** – a willingness and ability to identify and understand risks but not to take a risky approach in an unwise or reckless fashion.
- **Fairness** – a fair and open attitude which respects all human values.
- **Commitment** – an over-riding commitment to the project's success, user satisfaction and team working. A strong orientation towards goal achievement.

Introduction to the BoK

This *APM Body of Knowledge* (BoK) represents the topics in which practitioners and experts consider professionals in project management should be knowledgeable and competent. It has been derived from earlier versions updated and developed through an extensive research programme conducted by the Centre for Research in the Management of Projects (CRMP) at the University of Manchester Institute of Science and Technology (UMIST) on behalf of industry and the APM.

The scope of this *APM Body of Knowledge* incorporates not only inward focused project management topics, such as planning and control tools and techniques, but also those broader topics essential to the effective management of projects. These cover the context in which the project is being managed, such as the social and ecological environment, as well as a number of specific areas, such as technology, economics and finance, organisation, procurement, and people, as well as general management. Practice and research show these all have a significant influence on the likelihood of the project being conducted successfully [Morris, 1997].

The topics are described at a high level of generality. Detailed description of the topics can be found in texts, teaching and research institutions, companies, and other specific places. The intent here is principally to give an overall "scoping" guide to the topics that professionals in project management consider are essential for a suitable understanding of the discipline.

The topics are those that are *generic* to project management. The way they are described likewise is generic. Although ideas, language and even illustration may be derived from particular application, the intent is that each topic is potentially applicable in all project management situations.

Though intended as a generic guideline for project management, the BoK may come to be used, as other BoKs already are in many organisations, as the basis of the project management element of a general competencies framework.

The BoK is not a textbook. While it reflects what the research team and its advisors were able to discover to be the state of professional opinion (not just in the UK but with considerable input from outside the UK), the information presented has been filtered by the APM and the expertise of its members.

The topics have been grouped into seven sections.[2]
- The first section deals with a number of **General** and introductory items.

The remaining six sections deal with topics to do with managing:
- the project's **Strategic** framework, including its basic objectives;
- **Control** issues that should be employed;
- the definition of the project's **Technical** characteristics;
- the **Commercial** features of its proposed implementation;
- the **Organisational** structure that should fit the above;
- issues to do with managing the **People** that will work on the project.

(Though there is nothing fixed about this sequence, it is logical insofar as a strategic framework should first be established. The processes, practices and systems required for effective Control – in the sense of planning, reporting and taking corrective action – should be established from the outset. The project's technical definition should then be defined and developed with commercial conditions developed in parallel – but sometimes slightly lagging the technical definitional work. And then the organisational and people issues need to be factored in. These latter two are by no means the least important however: many consider, quite understandably, people issues to be at the very heart of successful project management.)

Many of the topics listed under these sections are closely linked or are interdependent. They are treated separately here however due to their individual significance. Teamwork and leadership for example, although they could be treated as a part of communications, are independently addressed due to their inherent importance in project management.

In reality, many of the topics fit in more than one section. Remember therefore that the categorisation is not intended to be too limiting. The section groupings are for convenience and clarity. But as in any sophisticated topic, high level groupings can become misleading. The granularity of the detail behind the ideas in this document is important.

---

2 For a long time we were reluctant to categorise the BoK topics into sections. Our surveys however showed a very strong desire for people to have a structure in which to group and provide a framework for the 40 odd topics. Research backs up the need for people to limit information without a structure of more than seven major topics [Miller, 1956]

The grouping of topics is shown in the diagram on the frontispiece. Each topic in the BoK has its own description together with a short list of useful references. (A list of Further References is additionally given at the end of the BoK.)

References

CURLING D H (ed), *"Project Management Body of Knowledge: Special Issue"*, **International Journal Project Management** 13 (2) April 1995

MORRIS, P W G, *"Bodies of Knowledge and Bodies of Competence"* **APM Yearbook**, APM, 1998

PROJECT MANAGEMENT INSTITUTE, *PMI Guide to the Body of Knowledge*, PMI, 1996

1 | General

This section covers a number of topics that need to be understood at the general level of project management which are not positioned under other sections.

The section starts with project management itself. Programme, Portfolio and other kinds of management are described. There is also discussion of the importance of fully understanding the context – the environment – within which the project is to be undertaken.

10 Project Management

Project Management is widely regarded as the most efficient way of introducing unique change. Essentially, project management achieves this by:

- defining what has to be accomplished, generally in terms of time, cost, and various technical and quality performance parameters;
- developing a plan to achieve these and then working this plan, ensuring that progress is maintained in line with these objectives;
- using appropriate project management techniques and tools to plan, monitor and maintain progress;
- employing persons skilled in project management – including normally a project manager – who are given responsibility for introducing the change and are accountable for its successful accomplishment.

Project Management is the discipline of managing projects successfully. Project Management can and should be applied throughout the project lifecycle, from the earliest stages of Concept definition into Operations & Maintenance, etc.[3] It comprises the management of all that is involved in achieving the project objectives safely and within agreed time, cost, technical, quality and other performance criteria. Project management provides the "single point of integrative responsibility" needed to ensure that everything on the project is managed effectively to ensure a successful project deliverable.

While projects should ideally be managed by a project manager this may not happen all the time. Whatever the title of the person, projects are most likely to be successful where someone has been clearly designated as accountable for its satisfactory accomplishment.

Typically projects involve several professionals working together and the project management expertise is spread across this team.

References

BRITISH STANDARDS INSTITUTE, *Guide to Project Management*, BSI: 6079, 1996

---

3 In most definitions of projects, the project is completed when it is turned over to Operations. However almost everyone recognises that cognisance needs to be taken of the Operations & Maintenance/ Integrated Logistics Support phase of operation. Planning input from this phase needs to be absorbed into the project and in many projects project, or programme , management will have some responsibility extended into the early period of start-up and operations. Indeed, many project professionals believe strongly that project management should also take cognisance of the Decommissioning stage of the product.

This diagram illustrates the project management process

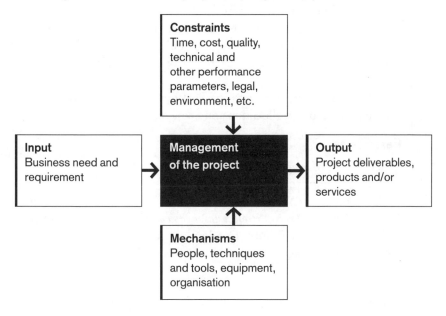

HARRISON F L, *Advanced Project Management*, Gower, 3rd edition, 1992

LOCK D, *Project Management*, Gower Publishing, 6th edition, 1996

MORRIS P W G, *The Management of Projects*, Thomas Telford, 1997

PINTO J K (ed), *The Project Management Institute: Project Management Handbook*, Jossey Bass, 1998

TURNER J R, The *Handbook of Project-Based Management*, 2nd edition, McGraw-Hill, 1999

11   Programme Management

There is widespread variation in the use of the term Programme Management. It can variously cover managing any or all of the following:

● a portfolio of projects related to some common objective;

● an organisation's business strategy which is to be implemented through projects;

● the interdependencies between a number of projects;

● resource allocation amongst a portfolio of projects.

The most common – and cogent – definition is that a programme is a collection of projects related to some extent to a common objective[4]. This could be a major project, a new business objective, a new product development, and so on. Programme Management is the effective management of that programme.[4]

Portfolio Management on the other hand is the management of a number of projects that do not share a common objective. An operations manager of a company managing several different projects for different clients would be an example.

Both Programme Managers and Portfolio Managers share similar problems of resource allocation and management.

References

BARTLETT J, *Managing Programmes of Business Change*, E & F N Spon, 1998

CCTA, *Managing Successful Programmes*, The Stationery Office, 1999

LOFTUS J edition (1999) *Project management of multiple projects and contracts* Thomas Telford: London

REISS G, *Programme Management Demystified*, E & F N Spon, 1996

12   Project Context

The successful accomplishment of a project generally requires a significant sensitivity to, and appreciation of, the context in which it is based.

Projects and their management both affect and are affected by their environment, often significantly. The project environment comprises both the internal and external environments in which the project is carried out. The project environment can be of various kinds – political, ecological (often termed environmental), economic, technological, regulatory, organisational, etc. These environments, or contexts, shape the issues that project management has to deal with and may assist or restrict the attainment of the project objective.

References

MORRIS P W G & HOUGH G H, *The Anatomy of Major Projects*, Wiley, 1987

BSI 6046 (part 1)

---

4 In some industries where projects or programmes are part of a much larger configuration of elements and systems, whose use in operation is particularly important and complex, terms associated with "Systems Management" and "Systems Acquisition" are also frequently used. Their use in general project management is limited however.

2 Strategic

The strategic framework provides the overall integrative framework for managing the project efficiently and effectively.

The strategic framework could cover many of the topics found elsewhere in this document, most particularly those found in Control. Almost all the topics in the BoK have a strategic element. Control, in the broader sense in which it is used in this BoK, clearly can have an important strategic dimension.

The topics that have been included in this section of the BoK are those that most obviously affect the strategic definition of the project.

20 Project Success Criteria

It is essential that the project's success criteria be clearly defined and agreed before significant development is initiated. These success criteria may be defined in a number of ways:

- Body of knowledge as business objectives (or goals),
- as "requirements",
- as Critical Success Factors or Key Performance Indicators, etc.

Terminology in this area is fluid. "Requirements" is generally taken to refer to technical [performance] requirements. Some people describe objectives as measurable targets leading to higher level goals; others take exactly the opposite view. "Critical Success Factors" are often used synonymously with "Key Performance Indicators", though normally KPIs are taken as the measures upon which the project will be judged when evaluating whether the project has been successful or not. "Critical Success Factors" are those measurable factors that, when present in the project's environment, are most conducive to the achievement of a successful project.[5]

"Key Performance Indicators"[6] describe those project management indicators that:

- are determined at the beginning of the project
- reflect directly on the key objectives [goals] of the project
- provide the basis for project management trade-off decisions during the course of the project.

At completion of the project these KPIs:

- will be the most relevant measures to confirm the acceptability of the project and its product by the project's stakeholders as being "successful";
- can be measured in some way, at some time, on some scale.

Establishing the project's fundamental success criteria at the outset – however they are termed – is absolutely one of the most important things

---

5 The definition of "success" is itself something that needs considerable care. Considerable work has done on this over the last decade or so [de Wit, 1987; Morris & Hough, 1987; Slevin & Pinto, 1988; etc.] It is important to realise that different parties on a project have different attitudes to, and measures of, success; and that these measures may give different results over time – as business conditions change for example.

6 Max Wideman of PMI Canada, in communication with CRMP, has suggested the term "Key Success Indicators" to describe these indicators. "Key Requirements Areas" is another commonly used term.

that must happen in order to ensure the successful realisation of a project. All projects are contextual and all have different success criteria. Defining and agreeing these from the outset will determine fundamentally how the project is to be managed and measured.

The success criteria should be documented and the manner in which it is proposed that they be achieved should be described. This is done in the project Strategy Plan (also variously termed the Project Management Plan, or even the Project Execution Plan, see Topic 21).

21 Strategy/Project Management Plan

The project's success criteria define what the project has to achieve and how its success will be evaluated. Key Performance Indicators and other metrics may be specified to define the measures by which this will be done.

The success criteria should be documented and the manner in which it is proposed that they be achieved should be described. Various terms are used to describe the resulting key document. The most common term used is the Project Management Plan. The term "Strategy Plan" may also be used. The Project Execution Plan (PEP) is another, although this often has more detailed connotation.[7]

The Project Management Plan is the most important document in the overall planning, monitoring, and implementation of a project. It is the baseline tool which should be used as a reference for managing the project. The project manager and his team should "own" it. The Plan should include a definition of overall objectives, statements on how these should be achieved (and verified), estimates of the time required and the budget, quality policy, Health, Safety and environmental policies, and risk management strategy. Other items of a technical, commercial, organisational, personnel or control nature might also be included.

The Project Management Plan establishes project management's interpretation of the why, what, how, who, how much, and when of the project. The "why" and "what" are management's statement of the success criteria. These should be agreed with the project sponsor – the owner of

---

7 Many consider that the Project Execution Plan follows the Strategy definition after the project has been defined sufficiently to be able to specify how the project is going to be carried out. The Strategy Plan, on the other hand, needs to be formulated from as early in the project as possible.

the project's business case – and as far as possible with other project stakeholders.[8]

The strategy for the project, the "how", covers major aspects of the project from concept to close out. These include the project manager's vision for the project – agreed with the sponsor of the business case – the tools and techniques to be used, the outline of the IT required, and some detail of the uniqueness of the change being introduced, together with a definition of how the deliverables are to be validated, used (operated) and handed over to the sponsor. Resources, finance, procurement, risk, technical issues and quality requirements will all be covered along with any other issues required to describe how the project is to be managed effectively.

Time management, including phasing,[9] will be included in "the when". Budgets and Cost matters define the "how much".

Both the project sponsor and the project manager and his/her team should formally accept the Plan. It should be reviewed periodically as the project goes through its formal review "gates"[10] and continuously updated at these points.

References

BRITISH STANDARDS INSTITUTE, *A Guide to Project Management*, BSI: 6079, 1996

MORRIS P W G, *The Management of Projects*, Thomas Telford, 1998

22 Value Management

"**Value** lies in achieving a balance between the satisfaction of many differing needs and the resources used in doing so. The fewer resources used or the greater the satisfaction of the need, the greater is the value"[11] At strategic level, it can be expressed in terms of costs vs benefits, parameters vs

---

8 The terms "Project Sponsor" and "Stakeholder" are discussed in more detail later in this Guide. (Topic 50)

9 The whole area of Time-to-Market and Concurrent Engineering – i.e. the use of mixed teams from different stages of the project in order to improve overall decision making and shorten project duration should be addressed strategically at an early stage of the project's definition.

10 The concept of review "gates" is discussed in Topic 60.

11 PrEN 12973 VM European Standard (endorsed by BSI).

objectives, expenditure vs needs, or investment vs outcome. Value may be defined in terms of worth. Another definition is the quotient: performance divided by cost.

Value Management is a structured means of improving "business decisions: increase effectiveness and enhance competitiveness".[12] It refers to the overall process of identifying key issues and setting targets in terms of success criteria; identifying the teams and processes necessary to achieve those; and reviewing these throughout the project to obtain successful results.

Value Management is concerned with the broader optimisation of strategic issues, generation of alternative courses of action and assessment of options. Generally Value Management consists of a series of structured workshops, facilitated by a value management specialist.

References

CONNAUGHTON J N, *Value Management in Construction: A client's Guide*, CIRIA, 1996

H M TREASURY, *Central Unit on Procurement: No. 54 Value Management*, H M Treasury, 1996

H M TREASURY; *Procurement guidance No 2: Value for money in construction procurement* HM Treasury 1998

MALE S, KELLY J, FERNIE M & BOWLES G, *The value management benchmark: A good practice framework for clients and practitioners* Thomas Telford: London, 1998

THIRY M, *Value Management Practice*, Project Management Institute, 1997

23 Risk Management

Risk Management covers the process of identification, assessment, allocation, and management of all project risks. Risks are present in all projects, whatever their size or complexity and whatever industry or business sector. Risks exist as a consequence of uncertainty. In project management terms, risks are those factors that may cause a failure to meet the project's objectives.

Project risk management recognises a formal approach to the process as opposed to an intuitive approach. Risks, once identified, assessed and

12   ibid.

allocated should be managed in order to minimise or completely mitigate their effect on a project. This may be achieved by developing either immediate or contingency responses to the identified risks. Such responses may remove, reduce, avoid, transfer, or accept the risks or lead to the abandonment of the project.

While risks are, according to the dictionary, associated with the possibility of failure, they may also be associated with opportunities.

The usual definition of a risk in project management is that the risk is the product of the probability of an event occurring times its impact if it did. Risk management should balance the upside opportunities with downside risks, doing so in an open, clear and formal manner. (And thus interacts with Value Management and Value Engineering – Topics 22 and 44 – and with the management of budgets and contingencies – Topic 33.)

References

CHapmAN C B & Ward S, *Project Risk Management*, Wiley, 1997

CHICKEN J, *The philosophy of risk*, Thomas Telford: London, 1998

ICE, *Risk analysis and management of projects*, Thomas Telford: London, 1998

SIMON P, *Project Risk Analysis and Management Guide (PRAM)*, APM Group, 1997

24 Quality Management

Quality refers, obviously, to more than just technical performance. Quality applies to everything in Project Management: Commercial, Organisation, People, Control, Technical, etc. Quality Management covers Quality Planning, Quality Control and Quality Assurance.

Quality Planning is the preparation, checking, and recording of actions that are necessary to achieve the standard of product or service that the customer and legislation requires.

Quality Control is the set of processes for planning and monitoring the project to ensure that quality is being achieved.

Quality Assurance is the set of processes and procedures required to demonstrate that the work has been performed according to the quality plan.

Total Quality Management is a much broader and more ambitious system (philosophy) for identifying what the client really wants, defining the organisation's mission, measuring throughout the whole process how well performance meets the required standards, and involving the total organisation in the implementation of a deliberate policy of continuous improvement.

References

DALE B G, *Managing Quality*, Prentice Hall, 1995

LEAVITT J S & Nann P C, *Total Quality Through Project Management*, McGraw Hill, 1994

ISO Series 9000,10000, and 11000 on Quality Assurance, Guides to the application of 9000 (see particularly 10006 on Quality in Projects, including the definition of the contents of the Project Management Plan), and Auditing

25   Health, Safety and Environment

"Health Safety, and Environment" involves determining the standards and methods required to minimise, to a level considered acceptable by the public, the legal system, users and operators, and others, the likelihood of accident or damage to people, equipment, property, or the environment.[13] This involves ensuring that these standards are respected and achieved in operation, and reviewing them to ensure their continued validity. It also entails proper appreciation of the legal and corporate environmental control and reporting procedures required for the project.[14]

References

CRONER, *Health and Safety in Practice: Health & Safety Manager*, Volumes 1 & 2.

DAVIES V J & TOMASIN K, *Construction Safety Handbook*, 2nd edition, Thomas Telford, 1996

ECI, *The ECI guide to managing health in construction*, Thomas Telford: London, 1999

STUBBS A, *Environmental law for the construction industry*, Thomas Telford: London, 1998

---

13 Although at first view it might be thought that "HS&E" does not apply in several project situations, our research showed that 100% across all sectors considered it applicable.

14 Note that the legal requirements of environmental legislation are specifically defined for different "environments", e.g. under ISO 14001 Guide to Environmental Management Systems.

3 Control

This section includes many of the core tools traditionally associated with project management.

A broad view of what is meant by Control is taken. Planning, measuring, monitoring and taking corrective action are all usually included in the Control cycle.[15] Effective planning determines how the project is to be approached. Monitoring and reporting then relates actual performance against these plans. Action may be needed to ensure performance is maintained. Re-planning may be necessary to ensure the project is accomplished successfully. All these together constitute control.

The heart of a planning and monitoring system is prediction and trend analysis based on reliable performance information. The project management professional should monitor the project against its baseline plan and Key Performance Indicators.

---

15 This is the classic definition of the control cycle derived form cybernetics – the science of communication and control.

30 Work Content and Scope Management

A fundamental aspect of effective project planning, and therefore of effective project management, is the processes of defining the scope of the project and of breaking this into manageable pieces of work (work packages). This can be achieved by first producing a scope definition (via Requirements Capture[16] etc.), then breaking the project scope into a product orientated hierarchy, i.e. a Product Breakdown Structure (PBS), and finally into a task orientated hierarchy, i.e. a Work Breakdown Structure (WBS).

The Scope definition describes what the product deliverables of the project are. (Managing this involves careful control of changes and deliverables – see Topic 46.)

The PBS is a product orientated hierarchical breakdown of the project into its constituent items without the tasks/work packaging being developed. The WBS is a task oriented detailed breakdown, which defines the work packages and tasks at a level above that defined in the networks and schedules. The WBS initiates the development of the Organisational Breakdown Structure (OBS), and the Cost Breakdown Structure (CBS). It also provides the foundation for determining Earned Value (see topic 35) and activity networks, and hence schedules (see topic 31).

References

BADIRU A A, *Project Management in Manufacturing and High Technology Operations*, Wiley, 1996

KERZNER H, *Project Management: A Systems Approach to Planning, Scheduling and Controlling*, 6th edition, Van Norstrand Rheinhold, 1997

MEREDITH J R & MANTEL S M, *Project Management*, Wiley, 1995

SHTUB A, BARD J F & GLOBERSSON S, *Project Management: Engineering, Technology and Implementation*, Prentice Hall, 1994

31 Time Scheduling/Phasing

The effective planning and accomplishment of activities' timing and phasing is a central skill of project management. Time scheduling/phasing comprises ordering the processes required to ensure timely completion of

16 Requirements Management is Topic 41.

the project. Scheduling consists of activity definition, activity sequencing, activity duration estimating, schedule development, and schedule control.

Phasing is more concerned with the strategic pacing of the project and the overlapping between different activities or blocks of activities. (For example, with the decision on whether or not to use Rapid Application Development prototyping, Concurrent Engineering, Simultaneous Design, Fast Track, Phased Hand-over, etc.) The phasing and overlapping of activities is also an important aspect of the project management team's skills. Properly done, it can have a major impact on the performance of the project (see Topic 60).

Activities are normally scheduled using techniques such as Bar charts (Gantt Charts, Milestone Charts) or networks (PERT, CPM, CPA, Precedence, Activity-on-Arrow, Activity-on-Node).[17] The concept of critical path is central to network scheduling. Resource Management also significantly affects this item.

References

Kerzner H, Project Management: *A Systems Approach to Planning, Scheduling and Controlling*, 6th edition, Van Norstrand Rheinhold, 1997
LOCKYER K G & GORDON J, *Project Management and Project Network Techniques*, Pitman, 6th edition, 1995
MEREDITH J R & MANTEL S M, *Project Management*, Wiley, 1995

32   Resource Management

Planning, allocating and scheduling resources to tasks, generally including people, machine (plant and equipment), money, and materials, is another fundamental requirement of effective project planning and management. Resource Management typically covers resource allocation and its impact on schedules and budgets, and resource levelling and smoothing.

33   Budgeting and cost management

The completion of the project within its budget is a central objective of project management. Budgeting and Cost Management is the process of

17 PERT: Program Evaluation Review Technique   CPM: Critical Path Method
    CPA: Critical Path Analysis.

estimating the proper cost that should reasonably be expected to be incurred against a clear baseline, understanding how and why actual costs occur, and ensuring that the necessary response is taken promptly to ensure actual costs come under budget. Successful cost management on a project needs to be forward-looking.

Typical information needed for cost management includes that on:
- budgets (including estimating), generally based on work breakdown structure or [cost] code of accounts;
- obtaining and recording commitments/accruals;
- measurement of work accomplished and value earned/valuation of work, including treatment of changes (change control) and claims;
- cash flow;
- forecast out-turn costs;
- variance analysis of the trend in forecast versus previous out-turn cost.

(Cost status should be linked with schedule status via Performance Measurement – see Topic 35, below, and of course with Quality.)

References

BENT J A & HUMPHEREYS K R, *Effective Project Management through Applied Cost and Schedule Control*, Dekker, 1996
SMITH N J (ed), *Project Cost Estimating*, Thomas Telford, 1995

34 Change Control

Almost all projects suffer change to their current "definition" at some point in their evolution. Changes may be proposed by any of the stakeholders associated with the project. Change may be unavoidable or highly desirable; it may equally be unnecessary and not useful. It is essential that any proposed change to the project be formally controlled. The project management team, with the support, as appropriate, of relevant stakeholders including the sponsor should therefore review changes fully before their approval and actioning. Their impact on all aspects of the project should be carefully assessed. All approved changes should be fully documented and efficiently communicated.

The project must have an effective change control system in operation and the project management professional should be familiar with its operation.

35   Earned Value Management

The term Earned Value[18] is a generic performance measurement term
for the concept of representing physical work accomplished in terms of
financial worth accrued[19].

Earned Value Management is the process of representing physical
progress achieved on the project in terms of a cost based measure (i.e.
money, or in some cases man hours). Cash measures of cost or quantity
measures of progress alone are not sufficient: serious distortions can
arise if physical progress is not related to financial progress in "value
earned" terms.

Various rules and techniques are used to represent the value of work
performed to date as a proportion of the total project value.

Structured estimates-to-complete are also given through Earned
Value based upon accurate assessment of status-to-date.

References

BRITISH STANDARDS INSTITUTION, *A Guide to Project Management*,
    BSI: 6079, HMSO, 1996
FLEMING, Q W, *Cost / Schedule Control Systems Criteria*, revised edition,
    Probus, 1993
FLEMING Q W & KOPPELMAN J M, *Earned Value Project Management*,
    PMI, 1996

36   Information Management

Projects generate and absorb significant quantities of information.
It is important that the project has an effective information management
system. Information management covers the management of the systems,
activities, and data that allow information in a project to be effectively
acquired, stored, processed, accessed, communicated, and archived.

---

18 In many organisations Cost / Schedule Control Systems Criteria (also known as
    C-SPEC) are used as a specific version of Earned Value.
19 Construction Bills of Quantities are a similar form of "performance measurement" since
    physical progress is measured in value earned terms, though they generally
    only apply to the site works portion of the project, and not to design or [overhead]
    management.

There should be a valid audit trail of this communication process. Document Management is another term frequently used in projects to cover aspects of Information Management.

Generally modern information and computer based technology can significantly impact the effective management of information. Ensuring a comprehensive, valuable IS – Information Systems – plan is available for the project as a whole should be an important responsibility of project management.

Information distribution involves making needed information available to project stakeholders in a timely manner. It includes implementing communication management plans as well as responding to unexpected requests for information.

4 | Technical

Effectively managing the technical definition of the project can make an enormous impact on its potential success. This is usually true even of seemingly non-technical projects such as some organisational change projects: all usually involve some definition of what has to be accomplished and how things are to work. Generally the technical base is both significant in size and importance.

The effective management of the technical base of the project involves ensuring, inter alia, that:

- the project's requirements are clearly stated;
- the technical base is elaborated with regard to the required quality, technical, safety, environmental and other standards;
- an appropriate technology strategy is in place;
- the design is value optimised;
- the work required is accurately estimated;
- implementation is effectively managed;
- testing plans and practices should be initiated from the outset;
- hand-over is effectively managed.

References

FORSBERG, K et al., *Visualising Project Management*, Wiley, 1996

MORRIS P W G, *The Management of Projects*, Thomas Telford, 1997

40 Design, Implementation and Hand-Over Management

Design is the activity of defining what is to be delivered. To a significant extent it will also influence how it will be made. It will obviously also determine extensively how it will be used. The design process needs to be effectively managed, ensuring particularly that there is:

- a clear statement of requirements, leading to a clear detailed definition of specifications;
- a proper constitution of the design team, with optimum input from all appropriate members of the project – marketing, production, etc.;
- a clear process plan and an optimum schedule, both for the design process itself and its relation with the rest of the project schedule;
- effective treatment of technology;
- effective modelling and testing;
- proper deployment of value management and value engineering practices, as well as clear input and control over project estimated out-turn costs;
- a clear definition of the scope of work to be included;
- effective change control, information management, and configuration management;
- a meeting of all planning, health, safety, environmental and other legislative requirements;
- proper management of the Hand-Over process (to Operations etc., or even straight to Decommissioning).

Many of these topics are covered explicitly in other sections of this Guide to the Project Management Body of Knowledge.

References

BADIRU A A, *Project Management in Manufacturing and High Technology Operations*, Wiley, 1996

MORRIS P W G, *The Management of Projects*, Thomas Telford, 1998

SHTUB A, *Project Management Engineering, Technology, and Implementation*, Prentice Hall, 1994

41 Requirements Management

Requirements management[20] covers the process of defining the user/customer requirements and building the system requirements

20 Brief preparation is also a term often used for this process.

set of requirements. Any changes to the initial requirements should be traceable (i.e. documented and explainable).

The requirements definition should be progressively updated as the project develops.

References

EISNER, H, *Essentials of Project and Systems Engineering Management*, Wiley, 1997

FORSBERG, K et al., *Visualising Project Management*, Wiley, 1996

STEVENS R et al., *Systems Engineering: Coping with Complexity*, Prentice Hall, 1998

42   Estimating

Accurately assessing the amount of work required to complete each work package (see topic 30) is fundamental in the definition of a project. The estimate usually begins as a quantification or measure of resource units required, which can then be translated into a financial budget using rate tables or actual costs. This topic is closely related to budgeting and cost management.

References

TURNER J R, *The Commercial Project Manager* Chapter 3, McGraw-Hill, 1995

LOCK D, *Project Management Handbook*, 6th edition Chapters 4 & 5, Gower, 1996

SMITH N, *Project Cost Estimating*, Thomas Telford, 1995

43   Technology Management

Where technology development is likely to be an issue in the future, or where operation of the product or interfacing technology or support

(e.g. "Pre-Planned Product Improvement
- technology compatibility/interfacing (e.g. GroupWare);
- operations support (e.g. Integrated Logistics Support).

Reference

SHTUB A, *Project Management: Engineering, Technology, and Implementation*, Prentice Hall, 1994

BLANCHARD B S, *Logistics Engineering and Management*, Prentice Hall, 1986

44 Value Engineering

At the technical level, value may be defined in terms of worth or the quotient: performance divided by cost where high performance and low cost are considered good value and low performance and high cost are bad value. "Achieving good value requires balancing a series of conflicting parameters to arrive at an optimum position".[22]

While Value Management is concerned with the broader optimisation of strategic issues, Value Engineering is concerned with optimising the conceptual, technical, operational and configuration aspects of value.

Value Engineering is the structured application of a series of proven techniques during the phases of a project when products are being developed. Considered, rightly, as an attitude of mind, formal Value Engineering involves a formal approach to the improvement of product solutions; it is achieved through teamwork in a workshop environment, using a job plan based on problem-solving and creative thinking.

References:

CONNAUGHTON J N, *Value Management in Construction: A client's Guide*, CIRIA, 1996

21 Technology Management might also cover Reliability, Maintainability, Availability (RMA) for example.
22 PrEN 12973 VM European Standard (endorsed by BSI).

HM TREASURY, *Central Unit on Procurement: No. 54 Value Management*,
HM Treasury, 1996

THIRY M, *Value Management*, Project Management Institute, 1997

45 Modelling and Testing

There are considerable benefits in both modelling the design and the
project deliverables as early in the project life cycle and as comprehensively
as possible. The project management professional should be technically
aware of the benefits and the costs of computer based modelling of the
design[23] together with other aspects of the project implementation and
should ensure that this happens in the most appropriate and cost effective
manner. Other forms of modelling commonly used include equipment/
software trials, demonstrators, and pilot runs.

The design and the evolving solution should be tested against the
requirements as it develops. Testing can take a variety of forms and
should be carried out effectively against the requirements definition.[24]
Techniques such as prototyping and rapid applications development
can be deployed as ways of testing the design prior to full implementation
authority being given.

Reference

GUSS C L, *"Virtual Project Management: Tools and the trade"*,
Project Management Journal, 29(1), pages 22–30, 1998.

46 Configuration Management

Configuration Management is the process of ensuring that the project
delivers everything it is supposed to – physical products and assets, quality
products, documentation, deliverables etc. – such that there is complete
assurance on delivery integrity. It is particularly concerned with managing
the status of pending and approved changes to the project deliverables

23 For example through CAD (Computer Aided Design)/ CAM (Computer Aided
Manufacturing), Virtual Engineering Environments and other forms of simulation.

24 Systems Engineers distinguish between Verification – testing to verify that a
requirement has been met – and Validation – assuring the product as a whole
performs integrally as required (Stevens et al, 1998).

and with managing the information that define the configuration status. (As such it is closely related to Change Control – see Topic 34.)

All project management deliverables (assets, documents, products) should be controlled such that there is complete assurance on delivery integrity.

References

BERLACK H R, *Software Configuration Management*, Wiley, 1992
CCTA, *Guide to Prince 2*, HMSO, 1996
ISO 10007, *Guidelines for Configuration Management*, 1995

5 Commercial

Commercial issues may drive the conduct of
the project.

50 Business Case

The business case defines why the project is required and what the change is to be.[25] The business case should include an outline of the project's objectives, deliverables, time, cost, technical, safety, quality and other performance requirements, and the major project risks and upside opportunities.

The business case might also include information on the competitive impact, resource requirements, organisational impacts, key performance indicators and critical success factors of the project and its outcome. The impact of these factors, together with the results of other forms of appraisal, such as environmental appraisal, social impact, etc, should be periodically assessed during the course of the project.

The same discipline should apply for supplier type companies considering bidding for work on a project as much as for project sponsors. Bidders should assess the business case of bidding for and winning (or losing) the project.

The sponsor, the person responsible for defining the business case and the development of the project against the business case, should "own" the business case.

The business case will generally form an extremely important proportion of the project's KPIs (see Topic 20).

The Business Case for the project, and its links to the project's justification, should be regularly reviewed. This will normally be done at key "Investment Gates" – which will often coincide with other formal strategic reviews.

Upon completion of the project there should be a formal evaluation of whether the project achieved its stated business benefits.

References

CORRIE R K (ed), *Project Evaluation*, Thomas Telford, 1990
TURNER JR, *The Commercial Project Manager*, McGraw-Hill, 1995

---

25 In general, both the Business Case and all major procurements should be subject to investment/business appraisal(s) in which the whole life cycle costs and all feasible options should be reviewed. The do–nothing option should always be considered. There will be occasions when the investment appraisal will show that the change will not represent value for money within the requirements defined.

51 Marketing and Sales

Marketing is the process of matching the abilities of an organisation with the existing and future needs of its customers, to the greatest benefit of both parties. The result is an exchange in which the organisation receives income through the meeting of customers' needs and customers receive benefits that satisfy their expectations.

Marketing is often of significant importance to project management professionals in that they can be involved in securing new business. This activity, important in itself, can also interact with the way a project is conceived and conducted.

Sales is the process of getting someone to buy the product or service being offered by the organisation. Some project management professionals can find themselves having to sell services or products. This too can significantly affect the way a project is conceived and managed.

52 FInancial Management

Financing the project is normally the sponsor's responsibility. The project management team should know, and be sensitive to, the impact of how the project is financed and the particular requirements imposed on the project by its financing. Particular attention is likely to be given to cash flow and to the value of early (or late) and/or on-time completion. Bonding requirements (financial, performance, etc) should be understood where appropriate. Currency fluctuations may be important where some or all funding is in foreign currency. Some understanding of the relationship between management accounting and project accounting/cost control is generally necessary.

References

HALEY G, *A–Z of BOOT*, IFR Publications, 1996
HUGHES W, Hillebrandt P & Murdoch J, *Financial protection in the UK building industry*, Thomas Telford: London, 1998
NEVITT P, *Project Financing*, Euromoney Publications, 1989

53 Procurement

Procurement is the process of acquiring new services or products.
It covers the financial appraisal of the options available, development
of the procurement or acquisition strategy, preparation of contract
documentation, selection and acquisition of suppliers, pricing, purchasing,
and administration of contracts. It may also extend to storage, logistics,
inspection, expediting, transportation, and handling of materials and
supplies. It may cover all members of the supply chain. Operations and
maintenance, for example, needs to be supported through a supply chain
management process.

For many projects, procurement can represent the highest percentage
of expenditure. It is essential that value for money is realised. All major
procurements should be subject to careful appraisal and management.
As with the business case, all feasible options should be considered.

A procurement strategy should be prepared very early in the project.
This will often stem from a policy defined externally to the project –
for example the urgency of the project. It will also often be a function
of the state of the project definition, and of the supplier market.
The procurement strategy could include potential sources of supply,
terms and types of contract/procurement,[26] conditions of contract,
the type of pricing, and method of supplier selection.

Project management professionals will often be involved in the
preparation and administration of contracts. As well as a firm
understanding of the contract[s] themselves, this will involve
definitions of risks and their mitigation (see Topic 23).

Reference

ASSOCIATION FOR PROJECT MANAGEMENT, *Contract Strategy for
Successful Project Management*, Association for Project Management,
1998

COX A. & TOWNSEND M, *Strategic procurement in construction*.
Thomas Telford: London, 1998

26 For example, "alignment" – as in Partnering or Alliancing – versus commodity
purchasing

54   Legal Awareness

Project management professionals should have an awareness of the
relevant legal duties, rights, and processes which govern in a particular
project situation. Selectively there should be an awareness of the potential
causes of disputes, liabilities, breaches of contract, means of resolving
a dispute, and legal basics of industrial relations.[27]

Reference

RUFF A, *Principles of Law for Managers*, Routledge, 1995

---

27 Statutory responsibilities, conditions of employment, and anti–discrimination
legislation etc.

6 Organisational

By "organisational" we mean here the structural aspects of the way the organisation is configured. (The people aspects are dealt with in the next section.)

The type of organisation in which, and by which, a project is managed should be appropriate to the project's Key Performance Indicators and Critical Success Factors (see Topic 20). This said, the form of organisation will strongly influence the way project management is to be applied.

60 Life Cycle Design and Management

The project life cycle describes the sequence of phases through which the project will evolve. It is absolutely fundamental to the management of projects. (The life cycle is the only thing that uniquely distinguishes projects from non-projects.)

Managing the evolution of the project through its life cycle is one of the most important skills of a project manager. The processes representing the project life cycle determine significantly how effectively the project is structured.

The basic life cycle follows a common generic sequence: Opportunity, Design and Development, Implementation, Hand-over, Post-Project Evaluation, etc. – although the exact wording often varies between industries and organisations.[28]

Effectively managing the life cycle ensures that issues will not be overlooked, time and money will not be wasted, and resources will be effectively deployed. There should be evaluation and approval points between phases. These are often termed "gates".[29]

The pacing and overlapping of phases, their staffing and their review and management is a central skill of project management. This is key for example in:

- optimising Time-to-market (and hence in areas such as Concurrent Engineering, Fast Track/ Fast Build, Phased Hand-over, Simultaneous Engineering, Rapid Application Development prototyping, etc.);
- strategic and design management reviews;
- Value Management and Cost Management.

Project life cycles can cover just the period up to the early stages of Operations and Maintenance.[30] However, some projects may have an extended life cycle, which can extend to the disposal or replacement of the product or service. Equally, new versions of products may be generated during Operations.

28 There is a significant variation in industry specific terminology for different phases of the life cycle. The basic sequence holds for all projects however, though enterprises bidding for project work will generally have Marketing and Bidding as the first two phases, whereas those investing in projects will typically have Concept and Feasibility as the first two.

29 There are "hard" gates and "soft" gates – the former implying absolutely that the project cannot proceed without formal management review and approval ; the latter implying a degree of option.

30 In some industries, particularly in the defence sector, Operations & Maintenance is termed Integrated Logistics Support.

It is common for some phases to be split into stages e.g. the concept phase can be divided into two stages, where the first stage would involve a wider range of options than the second stage which would investigate the proposed products or services in more detail.

The phases can be characterised as follows.

61   Opportunity

The Opportunity phase is often split into two stages.

In the first, Concept or Marketing, initial work on defining the opportunity should be enthusiastic and open-minded. Definitional work should be comprehensive – several different options should be investigated – and should lead to a full statement of the Strategy/ Project Management Plan (see Topic 21).

In the second, the opportunity should be subject to a thorough and critical review – should we go ahead with the investment/ should we bid; and if so, are we doing this in the optimal way? Generally during this stage, only one (or two) options will be investigated, but will be done so in detail. The aim should be to find ways of meeting the project objectives/KPIs more effectively, to check if the proposed way forward is feasible, and to understand the risks and opportunities associated with each potential option. Modelling of the options and their realisation should be as extensive as is cost effective.

The experience of project management has consistently shown that project personnel generally wish they had been more thorough and/or spent longer at the project "front end".

62   Design and Development

During this phase, detailed technical, commercial and organisational decisions are taken. There is often substantial opportunity to optimise these decisions without the expenditure of significant resource. Modelling, prototyping and testing may thus be effort well spent. Management approval gates will be necessary where major decisions are to be made – technical and design for example, or procurement and commercial.

In some industries this phase is dealt with as two separate phases with a management gate between the two. This is to allow the design to be developed in further outline before approval is given for significant resource expenditure on full design/development. Equally, the gate may be required before major procurement decisions and commitments are made after initial design but prior to full design/development.

63 Implementation

Implementation is the phase where the rate of resource expenditure is greatest. Planning should have ensured that this proceeds as efficiently as possible. There should normally be the minimum of changes in project definition at this stage.

64 Hand-Over

Hand-Over is the completion of the project to the satisfaction of the sponsor. It involves management of the introduction of the product or service being delivered by the project.

During Hand-Over, project records together with an audit trail documentation are completed and delivered to the sponsor. This documentation will be required at the post project evaluation review. All documentation should include any operations and maintenance plans.

There should also be a review of the original business case (Benefits Assessment) at this time, and/or in the next phase Post Project Evaluation.

65 (Post-) project evaluation review [O&M/ILS[31]]

Increasing recognition is being given to the importance of reviewing project performance and lessons that can be derived from the project. A post project evaluation review is carried once the operations phase has

---

31 Operations & Maintenance/ Integrated Logistics Support is the Product operations phase that succeeds Close-out. In some instances this is included within the remit of the project management team, to some degree at least. (De-commissioning is even included in some industries.) Usually, the project management activity concludes more or less with hand-over to operations. For this reason detail on the O&M/ILS phase has not been included. Preparation of the operations plan however might be a very important activity within the project.

started. The evaluation should cover all pertinent topics of the Guide to the Project Management Body of Knowledge.

Although often considered only after completion of the project, in practice Project Evaluation can and should be a fully integral part of the project. It should therefore be carried out periodically during the course of the project, with the resultant information/lessons fed back into this and other projects.

References

FORSBERG, K et al, *Visualising Project Management*, Wiley, 1996

MORRIS P W G, *The Management of Projects*, Thomas Telford, 1997

PINTO J K & SLEVIN D P, "*Critical Success Factors across the Project Life Cycle*", **Project Management Journal**, 19(3), pages 67–75, 1988

66 Organisation Structure

The project's organisation structure defines the reporting structures, processes, systems and procedures of the project. Issues typically important in the structuring of a project include the degree of project/functional orientation, the extent of the project management (office) authority, collocation of project members, the allocation of resources, work packaging and interface management, and the definition of control, authorisation and reporting procedures and systems.

There are three basic kinds of organisation structure:

- Functional – where resources are controlled totally from within their respective functional unit;
- Project – where resources are allocated on a dedicated basis to a project, from where they are controlled;
- Matrix – where resources are controlled functionally by their functional head and concerning their project requirements by the project manager[32].

The choice of structure should take account of cultural and environmental influences and may change as the project evolves through the project life cycle and because of different types and conditions of contract.

---

32 The term "Inverted Matrix" is sometimes used to describe the situation where functional managers support projects and project management teams.

References

PINTO J (ed.), *PMI Project Management Handbook*, Jossey- Bass, 1998

TURNER J R, GRUDE K V & THURLOWAY L, *The Project Manager as Change Agent*, McGraw-Hill, 1996

67 Organisational Roles

There are, or should be, various common roles found on projects. Examples include the following.

The **Project Sponsor** is the owner of the project business case. He/she represents the funder's interests.

A **Programme Manager** is generally responsible for the overall development of a product in its broadest sense. This may include in-service operation as well as related projects and tasks needed to ensure satisfactory development and delivery of the programme. (See Topic 11)

The **Project Manager** is responsible for delivering the project in the agreed schedule, to the correct technical specification (defined to meet user requirements), and within the approved budget and other specified criteria (Key Performance Indicators).

The **Project Support Office** supports the project through the examination of project status information and the provision of project help and support as may be required.

Other roles which appear frequently include that of the Project Board (called in some circumstances the Project Steering Committee), The Configuration Manager/Management Board, Project Planning/Planner, Cost Manager, Quality Manager, Resource Manager.

7 | People

This section addresses the so-called "soft" skills to do with managing people (which are in general very hard - that is, difficult). It also includes communications – communication can be an overriding activity for many managers.

70 Communications

Just as the project life cycle is fundamental to structuring the process of
project management, communication is fundamental to making it work.
Effective communication with all stakeholders is absolutely fundamental
to project success. Hence a communications plan is often developed at the
start of a project (see topic 36).

Communications can cover several media: oral, body language, written
(textural, numerical, graphic), paper, electronic, etc. The content and the
manner of delivery are perhaps more important however than simply the
medium.

Formal meetings are one important aspect of communication and can,
if not correctly managed, result in the waste of time, money and energy.
Certain meetings play a structural or process role in projects, for example,
the inaugural meeting which is required at project launch. Other meetings
include design reviews, periodic progress reviews, etc. The project
management professional should know what meetings are required when
in a project and how they should properly be conducted.

Information Management is also extremely important to effective
communications (see topic 36).

Reference

GUIRDHAM M, *Interpersonal Skills at Work*, Prentice Hall, 1995

71 Teamwork

Effective teamwork is generally at the heart of effective project
management. The project management professional should be familiar
with the process of forming a group of people into a project team that is to
work together for the benefit of the project. This can be achieved in a
formal manner by use of start-up meetings, seminars, workshops, etc. and
in an informal manner by getting the team to work well together.
Motivating and resolving conflicts between individual members of the
team are important elements of teamwork. Cultural characteristics of the
team members should be given full consideration: different cultures create
different working needs.

References

CORNICK T & Mather J, *Construction project teams:*
  Making them work profitably. Thomas Telford: London 1999
DINSMORE P C (ed.), *Human Factors in Project Management*,
  AMACOM, 1984

72 Leadership

Leadership is crucial in project management. Generally, project managers have to exercise considerable leadership skills. Management may be defined as the art of getting others to do what one cannot necessarily do oneself, by organising, controlling and directing resources. Leadership is the ability to identify what has to be done and then to select the people who are best able to tackle them. Leadership is about setting goals and objectives and generating enthusiasm and motivation amongst the project team, and stakeholders, to work towards those objectives.

Project leadership should be distinguished from the more particular roles of the project champion, who espouses the project and secures for it necessary support and resources, and the project sponsor, who is pre-eminently concerned with defining the project objectives in the context of the sponsoring organisation's other objectives. The sponsor is the holder of the business case.

References

DINSMORE P C (ed.), *Human Factors in Project Management*,
  AMACOM, 1984
GEDDES M, HASTINGS C & Brimer W, *Project Leadership*, Gower,
  2nd edition, 1996
PINTO J (ed.), *PMI Project Management Handbook*, Jossey-Bass, 1998.
TURNER J R, GRUDE K V, THURLOWAY L, *The Project Manager as
  Change Agent*, McGraw-Hill, 1996

73 Conflict Management

Conflict can occur at all levels in projects, largely because there may be many different parties working together with their own separate aims which at some point collide, or diverge. Projects, and contracts, easily engender conflict.

Conflict Management is the art of managing and resolving conflict creatively and productively. The art of conflict management is to channel these conflicts so that the result is positive, preferably synergistically so, rather than destructive.

References

THAMHAIN H J & WILEMAN D L, *"Leadership Conflict and Project Management Effectiveness"*, **Sloan Management Review**, Fall 1987

PINTO J (ed.), *PMI Project Management Handbook*, Jossey-Bass, 1998

74 Negotiation

All projects will involve the need for negotiation. The art of negotiation is in achieving to the greatest extent possible what you want from a transaction while leaving all parties sufficiently content that the relationship subsequently works well.

Reference

PINTO J (ed.), *PMI Project Management Handbook*, Jossey- Bass, 1998

75 Personnel Management

The management of personnel factors is often a significant element of project management. This may include recruiting, identifying labour and staff skill requirements and availability, developing training and development requirements, dealing with workforce disputes, and health and welfare issues.

While many if not most of these matters require specialist knowledge and skills, the project management professional should be knowledgeable of their relevance.

Further Reading References

10 Project Management

BRADLEY K, *Understanding PRINCE 2*, Butterworth-Heinemann, 1997

BRITISH STANDARDS INSTITUTE, *Guide to Project Management*, BSI: 6079, 1996

DINSMORE P C (ed.), *The AMA Project Management Handbook*, AMACOM, 1994

HAMILTON A, *Management by Projects*, Thomas Telford, 1997

MEREDITH J R & Mantel S J, *Project Management: a Managerial Approach*, 3rd edition, Wiley, 1995

SMITH N J, *Engineering Project Management*, Blackwell Science Ltd, 1995

TURNER J R, GRUDE K V, & THURLOWAY L, *The Project Manager as Change Agent*, McGraw-Hill, 1996

WOODWARD J F, *Construction project management: getting it right first time*, Thomas Telford, 1997

11 Programme Management

BARTLETT J, *Managing Programmes of Business Change*, Today Publications

BUTTRICK R, *The Project Workout*, Pitman, 1997

GRAY R J, "Alternative approaches to programme management", *International Journal of Project Management*, 15(1), pages 5–9, 1997

LOFTUS J E (ed.), *Project Management of Multiple Projects and Contracts*, Thomas Telford Publishing, 1999

PAYNE J H, "*Management of Multiple Simultaneous Projects: a State of the Art Review*", **International Journal of Project Management**, 13(3), pages 163, 1995

PELLEGRINELLI S, "*Programme Management: Organising Project Based Change*", **International Journal of Project Management**, 15(3), pages 141–150, 1997

TURNER J R, GRUDE K V & THURLOWAY L, *The Project Manager as Change Agent*, McGraw-Hill, 1996

VAN DE MERWE A P, "*Multi-project management – Organisational structure and control*", **International Journal of Project Management**, 15(4), pages 223–233, 1997

WHEELWRIGHT S C, & Clark K B, "*Creating project plans to focus product development*", **Harvard Business Review**, 70(2), pages 70–82, 1992

12 Project Context

CLELAND & KING, *Project Management Handbook*, 2nd edition, Van Nostrand Reinhold, 1988
TURNER J R, *The Commercial Project Manger*, McGraw Hill, 1995
TURNER J R, The *Handbook of Project-Based Management*, 2nd edition McGraw-Hill, 1999

20 Project Success Criteria

CLELAND & KING, *Project Management Handbook*, 2nd edition, Van Nostrand Reinhold, 1988
FIELD M & KELLER L, *Project Management*, The Open University
KERZNER H, *Project Management: A Systems Approach to Planning, Scheduling and Controlling*, 5th edition, Van Nostrand Reinhold, 1995
TURNER J R, *The Handbook of Project-Based Management*, 2nd edition McGraw-Hill, 1999

21 Strategy/Project Management Plan

CLELAND & KING, *Project Management Handbook*, 2nd edition, Van Nostrand Reinhold, 1988

22 Value Management

BRITISH STANDARDS INSTITUTE, *Value Management*, PrEN 12973

23 Risk Management

BALDRY D, "*The evaluation of risk management in public sector capital projects*", **International Journal of Project Management**, 16(1), pages 35–41, 1998
CHapmAN R J, "*The effectiveness of working group risk identification and assessment techniques*", **International Journal of Project Management**, 16(6), pages 333–343, 1998
THOMPSON P A & PERRY J G (eds.), *Engineering Construction Risks – A Guide to Project Risk Analysis and Risk Management*, 2nd edition, Thomas Telford, 1998

24 Quality Management

BRITISH STANDARDS INSTITUTE, *Quality management – Guidelines for Quality Plans*, BS ISO 10005, 1995

WOODWARD J F, *Construction Project Management – Getting it right first time*, Thomas Telford, 1997

25 Health, Safety and Environment

BRITISH STANDARDS INSTITUTE, *Occupational Health and Safety Management Systems*, OHSAS 18001, 1999
BRITISH STANDARDS INSTITUTE, *Environmental Management Systems*, BS EN ISO 14001, 1996
TURNER J R, GRUDE K V & THURLOWAY L, *The Project Manager as Change Agent*, McGraw-Hill, 1996

30 Work Content and Scope Management

REISS G, *Programme Management Demystified*, E & F N Spon, 1996

31 Time Scheduling / Phasing

BADIRU A A, *Project Management in Manufacturing and High Technology Operations*, Wiley, 1996
FIELD M & KELLER L, *Project Management*, The Open University
LEWIS J P, *Project Planning, Scheduling & Control*, Probus, 1995
O'CONNOR J T & NORWICH W, *"Fossil power plant schedule compression tactics: lessons from independent power producers"* **Project Management Journal**, 24(3), pages 34–42, 1993
TURNER J R, *The Handbook of Project-Based Management*, 2nd edition McGraw-Hill, 1999
SKELTON T M & THAMHAIN H J, *"Concurrent project management: a tool for technology transfer, R&D-to-market"* **Project Management Journal**, 24(4), pages 41–48, 1993
STALK G. & HOUT T M, *Competing Against Time*, Free Press, 1990

32 Resource Management

BELOUT A, *"Effects of human resource management on project effectiveness"*, **International Journal of Project Management**, 16(1), pages 21–26, 1998
FIELD M & KELLER L, *Project Management*, The Open University
LESTER A, *Project Planning and Control*, 2nd edition, Butterworth Heinemann, 1991

33 Budget and Cost Management

BARNES N M L (ed.), *Financial Control*, Thomas Telford, 1990
BRANDON D M, *"Implementing earned value easily and effectively"*, **Project Management Journal**, 29(2), pages 11–18, 1998

CLARK F D, *Applied Cost Engineering*, 3rd edition, Dekker, 1997
HUMPHREYS K R, *Basic Cost Engineering*, 3rd edition, Dekker, 1996
SMITH N J, *Engineering Project Management*, Blackwell Science, 1995

34 Change Control

LOCK D, Project Management, Gower, 1996

35 Earned Value Management

LESTER A, *Project Planning and Control*, 2nd edition, Butterworth
Heineman, 1991
ROBINSON P B, "*The performance measurement baseline – a statistical view*",
Project Management Journal, 28(2), pages 47–52, 1997
SHENHAR A J, "*Mapping the dimensions of project success*", **Project
Management Journal**, 28(2), pages 5–13, 1997
SMITH N J, *Engineering Project Management*, Blackwell Science, 1995

36 Information Management

CLELAND & KING, *Project Management Handbook*, 2nd edition, Van
Nostrand Reinhold, 1988
KERZNER H, *Project Management: A Systems Approach to Planning,
Scheduling and Controlling*, 5th edition, Van Nostrand Reinhold, 1995
LAUDEN & LAUDEN, Information Systems – A Problem solving Approach,
The Dryden Press, 1995

40 Design, Implementation and Hand-Over Management

CHATZOGLOW P D & MACAULAY L A, "*The Importance of Human Factors in
Planning the Requirements Capture Stage of a Project*", **The International
Journal of Project Management**, 15(1), 1997, pages 39–54
CLELAND D I, "*Product Design Teams: The simultaneous engineering
perspective*" **Project Management Journal**, 22(4), pages 5–10, 1991
THAMHAIN H J, *Engineering Program Management*, Wiley 1984
WEARNE S H, "*Project design flexibility*", **Engineering Management
Journal**, 2 (5), pages 232–236

42 Estimating

KERZNER H, *Project Management: A Systems Approach to Planning,
Scheduling and Controlling*, 5th edition, Van Nostrand Reinhold, 1995
LOCK D, Project Management, Gower, 1996

TURNER J R, *The Commercial Project Manager*, McGraw Hill, 1995
SMITH N, *Project Cost Estimating*, Thomas Telford, 1995

44 Value Engineering

INSTITUTION OF CIVIL ENGINEERS, *Creating Value in Engineering
    Projects*, Thomas Telford, 1996
WILD R, *Production and Operations Management*, 4th edition, Cassell, 1989

45 Modelling and Testing

STEVENS R et al, *Systems Engineering: Coping with Complexity*,
    Prentice Hall, 1998

46 Configuration Management

ALLAN G, "*Configuration management and its impact on businesses that use
    computer platforms*", **International Journal of Project
    Management**, 15(5), pages 321–330, 1997
FORSBERG K et al, *Visualising Project Management*, Wiley, 1996
TURNER J R, The *Handbook of Project-Based Management*, 2nd edition
    McGraw-Hill, 1999

50 Business Case

LANG H J, & MERINO D N, *Selection Process for Capital Projects*,
    Wiley, 1993
SOUDER W E, *Project Selection & Economic Appraisal*, Van Nostrand
    Reinhold, 1993
TURNER J R, *The Commercial Project Manager*, McGraw Hill, 1995

52 Financial Management

BUTTRICK R, *The Project Workout*, Pitman, 1997
FIELD M & KELLER L, *Project Management*, The Open University
MCCARTHY S C & TIONG R L K, "*Financial and contractual aspects of
    build-own-operate-transfer projects*" **International Journal of Project
    Management**, 9(4), pages 222–227, 1991
MERNA A & DUBEY G E, *Financial Engineering in the Procurement
    of Projects*, Asia Law & Practice, 1998
SMITH N J, *Engineering Project Management*, Blackwell Science, 1995
TURNER J R, *The Commercial Project Manager*, McGraw Hill, 1995

53 Procurement

CLELAND & KING, *Project Management Handbook*, 2nd edition, Van Nostrand Reinhold, 1988

HOLT G D, *"Which contractor selection methodology?"* **International Journal of Project Management**, 16(3), pages 153–164, 1998

KERZNER H, *Project Management: A Systems Approach to Planning, Scheduling and Controlling*, 5th edition, Van Nostrand Reinhold, 1995

LARSON E, *"Barriers to project partnering: report from the firing line"*, **Project Management Journal**, 28(1), pages 46–52, 1997

LOCK D, Project Management, Gower, 1996

SMITH N J, *Engineering Project Management*, Blackwell Science, 1995

TURNER, J R, *The Commercial Project Manager*, McGraw Hill, 1995

WEARNE S H, & WRIGHT D, *"Organizational risks of joint ventures, consortia and alliance partnerships"*, **International Journal of Project & Business Risk Management**, 2(1), pages 45–57, 1998

54 Legal Awareness

JENSEN D, *"Seven legal elements for a claim for construction acceleration,"* **Project Management Journal**, 28(1), pages 32–44, 1997

TURNER J R, *The Commercial Project Manager*, McGraw Hill, 1995

60 Life Cycle Design and Management

BRITISH STANDARDS INSTITUTE, *Guide to Project Management*, BSI: 6079, 1996

O'CONNOR J T & Norwich W, *"Fossil power plant schedule compression tactics: lessons from independent power producers"* **Project Management Journal**, 24(3), pages 34–42, 1993

SKELTON T M & THAMHAIN H J, *"Concurrent project management: a tool for technology transfer, R&D-to-market"* **Project Management Journal**, 24(4), pages 41–48, 1993

TURINO J, *Simultaneous Engineering – buying time to market*, Van Norstrand Rheinhold, 1992

63 Implementation

CUSUMMANO & NOBEKA, *Thinking Beyond Lean*, Free Press, 1998

RUSINKO C, *"Design-manufacture integration to improve new product development"*, **Project Management Journal**, 28(2), pages 37–46, 1997

65 (Post-) Project Evaluation Review

CORRIE R K (ed.), *Project Evaluation*, Thomas Telford, 1991
BLANCHARD B S, *Logistics Engineering and Management*,
Prentice Hall, 1986

66 Organisation Structure

CLELAND D I, *Project Management Handbook*, Van Nostrand
Rheinhold, 1993
El-NAJDAWI M K, *"Matrix management effectiveness: An update for research
and engineering organizations"*, **Project Management Journal**, 28(1),
pages 25–31, 1997
FLEMING Q W, *"Integrated project development teams: Another fad …
or a permanent change?"*, **Project Management Journal**, 28(1),
pages 4–11, 1997
FRAME J D, *Managing Projects in Organizations*, Jossey-Bass, 1995
GOBELI D & LARSON E W, *"Relative Effectiveness of Different Project
Structures"*, **Project Management Journal**, 18(2), pages 81–85, 1987
KERZNER H, *Project Management: A Systems Approach to Planning,
Scheduling and Controlling*, 5th edition, Van Nostrand Reinhold, 1995
TURNER J R, GRUDE K V & THURLOWAY L, *The Project Manager as
Change Agent*, McGraw-Hill, 1996

70 Communication

APM, Standard Terms for the Appointment of a Project Manager,
Association for Project Management, 1998
CIB, *Project Management Skills*, Construction Industry Council, 1996
CLELAND D I, *"Project stakeholder management"*, **Project Management
Journal**, 17(4), pages 36–44, 1986.
KERZNER H, *Project Management: A Systems Approach to Planning,
Scheduling and Controlling*, 5th edition, Van Nostrand Reinhold, 1995
LAUDEN & LAUDEN, Information Systems – A Problem solving
Approach, The Dryden Press, 1995
PINTO J (ed.), *PMI Project Management Handbook*, Jossey-Bass, 1998
YOUNG T L, *How to be a Better Communicator*, Kogan Page, 1996

71 Teamwork

BEE R & BEE F, *Project Management: The People Challenge*, Institute of
Personnel & Development, 1997
BELBIN, *Management Teams*, Butterworth-Heinemann, 1994

CLELAND D I (ed.), *Global Project Management Handbook*,
McGraw Hill, 1996
CLELAND D I, *"Product Design Teams: The simultaneous engineering
perspective"* **Project Management Journal**, 22(4), pages 5–10, 1991
HOFSTEDE G, *Cultures and Organisations: Software of the Mind*,
McGraw Hill, 1993
HOFSTEDE G, *"Cultural dimensions for project management"* **International
Journal of Project Management** 1(1), pages 41–48, 1983
KATZENBACH J R & SMITH D K, *The wisdom of teams: creating
high-performing organisations*, Harvard Business School, 1993
KLIEM R L & LUDIN I S, *The People Side of Project Management*,
Gower, 2nd edition, 1995
PINTO J K & KHARBANDA O P, *Successful Project Managers: Leading
your Team to Success*, Van Nostrand Reinhold, 1995
RANDOLPH, W A & POSNER B Z, *Getting the Job Done: Managing Project
Teams and Tasks Forces for Success*, Prentice Hall, 1992
TAMPOE M & THURLOWAY L, *"Project management: the use and abuse of
techniques and teams (reflections from a motivation and environment study)"*
International Journal of Project Management, 11(4), pages
245–250, 1993
TURNER J R, GRUDE K V & THURLOWAY L, *The Project Manager as
Change Agent*, McGraw-Hill, 1996

72 Leadership

CLELAND & KING, *Project Management Handbook*, 2nd edition,
Van Nostrand Reinhold, 1988
DINSMORE P C, (ed.), *Handbook of Program & Project Management*,
AMACOM, 1988.
FIELD M & KELLER L, *Project Management*, The Open University
KLIEM R L & LUDIN I S, *The People Side of Project Management*, Gower,
2nd edition, 1995
KOUZES J M & POSNER B Z, *The Leadership Challenge: How to get
Extraordinary Things Done in Organisations*, Jossey Bass, 1995
TURNER J R, GRUDE K V & THURLOWAY L, *The Project Manager as
Change Agent*, McGraw-Hill, 1996

73 Conflict Management

PINTO J K, *"Project management and conflict resolution"*, **Project
Management Journal**, 26(4), pages 45–54, 1995

74 Negotiation

FIELD M & KELLER L, *Project Management*, The Open University

FISHER R, Or W & Patton B, *Getting to Yes: Negotiating Agreement Without Giving In*, Penguin, 1991

RUSKIN A M & ESTES W E, *What Every Engineer Should Know About Project Management*, Marcel Dekker, 2nd edition, 1995, Chapter 9

Comparison with Previous Version

Areas of significant difference compared with the previous version of
the APM BoK (1996 edition) include:
- Tighter definition of Success Criteria.
- Value Management split from Value Engineering, because VM is
  Strategic and VE is basically technical/configuration/engineering.
- All the topics in the technical section are new, except for VE,
  Estimating and Configuration Management (previously combined
  with Change Control).
- Better definition of Procurement.
- Better coverage of Life Cycle Design and Management.
- Organisational Roles in addition to Organisation Structure.

In addition, several topics in the previous version have been incorporated
into other topics or omitted entirely:
- System Management – omitted as not sufficiently understood
  or relevant.
- Project Appraisal – incorporated in Business Case and Financial
  Management.
- Integration – incorporated in Project Management.
- Control & Co-ordination – incorporated in the whole section
  on Control.
- Delegation – omitted as not sufficiently substantial.
- Management Development – incorporated in Personnel Management.
- Mobilisation – omitted as covered in Resource Management and
  Personnel Management.
- Operation/Technical Management – incorporated in the whole section
  on Technical.
- Industrial Relations – incorporated in Personnel Management.